D1267155

WILD WHEELS
PORSCHES

By Heather Moore Niver

Gareth Stevens
Publishing

Please visit our website, www.garethstevens.com. For a free color catalog of all our high-quality books, call toll free 1-800-542-2595 or fax 1-877-542-2596.

Library of Congress Cataloging-in-Publication Data

Niver, Heather Moore.
Porsches / Heather Moore Niver.
    p. cm. — (Wild wheels)
Includes bibliographical references and index.
ISBN 978-1-4339-5840-3 (pbk.)
ISBN 978-1-4339-5841-0 (6-pack)
ISBN 978-1-4339-5838-0 (library binding)
1. Porsche automobiles—Juvenile literature. I. Title.
TL215.P75N58 2012
629.222—dc22

2011011925

First Edition

Published in 2012 by
Gareth Stevens Publishing
111 East 14th Street, Suite 349
New York, NY 10003

Copyright © 2012 Gareth Stevens Publishing

Designer: Daniel Hosek
Editor: Kristen Rajczak

Photo credits: Cover and interior pages (background), cover (Porsche), pp. 1, 14–15, 26–27 Shutterstock.com; pp. 4–5 Johanna Leguerre/AFP/Getty Images; pp. 6–7 Car Culture/Getty Images; p. 6 (Ferdinand Porsche and son) Keystone/Hulton Archive/Getty Images; pp. 8–9 Juergen Schwarz/Getty Images; pp. 10–11 Joel Saget/AFP/Getty Images; pp. 12–13 Hannelore Foerster/Bloomberg/Getty Images; p. 15 (Porsche symbol) Sean Gallup/Getty Images; pp. 16–17 Matt Campbell/AFP/Getty Images; pp. 18–19 Bryan Mitchell/Getty Images; pp. 20–21 Darrell Ingham/Getty Images; pp. 22–23 Sean Greenwood/Getty Images; pp. 24–25 RB/Redferns/Getty Images; p. 27 (Jerry Seinfeld) Valery Hache/AFP/Getty Images; pp. 28–29 Stan Honda/AFP/Getty Images.

Printed in the United States of America

CPSIA compliance information: Batch #CS11GS: For further information contact Gareth Stevens, New York, New York at 1-800-542-2595.

CONTENTS

Words in the glossary appear in **bold** type the first time they are used in the text.

Porsche Pride

Few cars shout "sports car!" like a Porsche. Since the first model was introduced in the 1940s, Porsches have been known for classy looks and, of course, speed! They have nearly spotless standing in the car world and are considered some of the finest cars on the road.

Many classic Porsches are on display at the Porsche Museum in Stuttgart, Germany.

Despite the fame of these cars, many people still don't know how to say their name. It's pronounced "POHR-shuh."

Porsche's long history as an independent company—one not owned by a bigger company—has been a source of pride for the German carmaker. Independence gives a company freedom to **design** cars however it wants. And has Porsche ever designed well!

INSIDE THE MACHINE

In 2009, a museum built just to show Porsches opened in Germany. It features examples of Porsche sports cars and race cars that have been made through the years. A workshop lets visitors watch Porsches being repaired. There are special tours for kids and even a restaurant!

The First Porsche

In 1900, Ferdinand Porsche and Jacob Lohner displayed an electric **carriage** called the System Lohner-Porsche at the World's Fair in Paris, France. They had been making carriages since 1898.

When the first Porsche model was produced in 1948, it was based heavily on the Volkswagen (VW). Ferdinand Porsche had designed for the VW company in the 1930s. He and his son, Ferdinand "Ferry" Anton Ernst Porsche, designed Porsches together until 1950.

Ferdinand Porsche and his son

INSIDE THE MACHINE

In 1934, Porsche designed a tractor. Porsche tractors used the same kind of engine for every model until the last one in 1963. During World War II, Ferdinand and his son, Ferry, worked on tank designs, too!

This carriage designed by Porsche and Lohner was a **hybrid**.

The Speedster

On June 8, 1948, the first Porsche 356 was approved for road driving. It's sometimes called the cousin of the VW because they were so similar. For example, both had engines cooled by air and located in the rear of the car. By the end of 1955, Porsche had produced more than 7,600 of the 356.

In the early 1950s, Porsche introduced a 356 model called the Speedster. Drivers could choose a **coupe** or a **convertible**. The coupes had hard tops and the convertibles, which they called cabriolets, had soft tops.

This 1954 Porsche 356 Speedster was at a classic car show in Germany in 2006.

INSIDE THE MACHINE

To celebrate its 60th anniversary, the Porsche company searched for the oldest Porsches sold in America. The winner was a bright red 1952 Porsche 356 Cabriolet that was owned by a man in Oklahoma. A blue 1950 356 Cabriolet was found in Maryland, but it was originally sold in Germany.

The 911

In the 1960s, Porsche introduced the 911. It was an immediate hit! Porsche has been making it ever since. The body style has changed through the years, but the engine has always been in the rear. The 1967 911 Targa featured a **roll bar** beneath a steel cover. The top between the roll bar and the windshield could be folded up and removed.

In early 2011, Porsche announced plans for a special 2012 Black Edition 911. This model came in black, inside and out. Porsche only made 1,911 of this special edition.

The Porsche 911 has been a classic model through five decades . . . and counting!

INSIDE THE MACHINE

In 1975, Porsche added another edition of the 911—the Turbo Carrera. Porsche added a **turbocharger** to see if it could make the car go faster. It worked! The car was so different from the 911 that it was given its own number: 930.

The 914

In the 1970s, Porsche worked with VW again and rolled out the 914 model. They wanted to make a car that more people could afford. However, the 914 wasn't well received, and some didn't even consider it a "real" Porsche. The 914 had a Targa-style roll bar, which many thought looked like a "basket handle." It also had a **mid-ship engine** made by VW. The 914/6 had a Porsche engine, but it didn't sell well either. Still, the 914 and 914/6 won *Motor Trend* magazine's Import Car of the Year contest.

Mid-engine cars were popular on the racetrack when the 914 was introduced. These "middies" had the engine right behind the driver and passengers of the car instead of in the front or at the rear. An engine produces a lot of heat, noise, and movement, and the 914 never had enough padding between it and the people in the car.

The Porsche 914/8 was first produced in honor of Ferry Porsche's 60th birthday.

The 928 and the 944

In the late 1970s, Porsche started to worry that its most popular model, the 911, would become outdated or be taken off the road because of safety concerns about rear-engine cars. The 928 was supposed to replace the 911. It was the first Porsche designed with the engine in the front of the car. However, 911s continued to sell well.

In 1982, the first 944 hit the highways. The 944 Turbo zipped up to 60 miles (97 km) per hour in less than 6 seconds and reached a top speed of 155 miles (249 km) per hour.

The Porsche 928 was sold from 1978 to 1995.

In 1952, Ferry Porsche drew the company logo on a napkin. It shows a **symbol** of Stuttgart, Germany, the city in which Porsche manufactures its cars. A horse is included because the city was built on an old horse farm. The antlers and the red and black stripes stand for the old Kingdom of Württemberg, Germany.

The Boxster

Times were tough in the 1990s, and excitement over Porsches was slowing. Enter the Boxster in 1997. Everyone loved it! It was a two-seat **roadster** with a six-**cylinder** engine known as a "boxer" that was cooled with water. The Boxster reminded car lovers of the classic Porsches from the 1950s. Porsche combined the words "boxer" and "roadster" to come up with the name.

Automobile magazine named the Boxster its Automobile of the Year in 1998.

Encouraged by the Boxster's success, Porsche decided to produce a more powerful model. In 2000, Porsche introduced a super (S) model with more power, the Boxster S. The Boxster S could speed from 0 to 60 miles (97 km) per hour in only 5.9 seconds!

INSIDE THE MACHINE

The Porsche Cayman is a coupe modeled after the Boxster. The name "Cayman" supposedly refers to an alligator-like reptile from Central and South America. Like the Boxster, the Cayman is a mid-engine car designed to be more affordable.

A Porsche SUV?

Many Porsche fans grumbled when the great sports car company put its name on a sport utility vehicle (SUV). But when Porsche offered the Cayenne—named after a hot pepper—in 2003, many doubters liked its spice. The 2006 Cayenne Turbo S could reach 60 miles (97 km) per hour in 4.9 seconds!

Although it was less sleek than Porsche's sporty cars, the Cayenne was sturdy. It had more space than Porsche cars but less than other mid-size SUVs. Excellent steering and **all-wheel drive** appealed to sports-car fans. The Cayenne offered several different engines that provided a range of power.

INSIDE THE MACHINE

Porsche didn't offer a Cayenne in the 2007 model year, but for 2008 this SUV was much improved. Several engines were still available, and every one of them provided more power than before. In 2011, Porsche introduced a hybrid model.

The Cayenne shares its frame and doors with another SUV—the VW Toureg.

Motor Sports

Porsche has been in the racing game for more than 50 years. Almost every series model has started out as a race car. Porsches have won 14 team world championships, 8 long-distance world titles, and many other races and championships. Porsches have won more Rolex Series races than the cars of any other maker.

Joerg Bergmeister drives the Porsche 911 GT3 before the American Le Mans Series Monterey Sports Car Championship in 2008.

In 2003, a Porsche 911 GT3 RS won the Rolex 24 at Daytona in Florida. This 24-hour race takes place at the Daytona International Speedway on a track that uses part of the NASCAR oval and part of an infield road course. The 911 was driven by Kevin Buckler from California, Michael Schrom from New York, and German Porsche racing stars Timo Bernhard and Joerg Bergmeister.

INSIDE THE MACHINE

Porsche race cars were a force on the 1980s racing scene. The 956 and the 962 won five team, manufacturers, and drivers world championships between 1982 and 1989. They also won six Le Mans races.

In 2010, Porsche introduced the 911 GT3 Cup car. It was based on the best-selling 911 GT3 RS road car. The GT3 Cup racer was built for the track. It won the 2011 Rolex 24 at Daytona, which was the 73rd win for Porsche.

The GT3 Cup car had a wide body, so there was room for wider wheels and tires. The six-cylinder engine was even more powerful than the GT3 RS. Better **ventilation** made sure that the driver got a lot more fresh air during a race. It was only made in the color Porsche calls "Carrara White."

The Porsche 911 GT3 Cup car races during the Rolex 24 at Daytona, January 29, 2011.

INSIDE THE MACHINE

Actor, director, and activist Paul Newman owned and raced Porsches. Newman must have talked about racing a lot. Costar Robert Redford once gave him a dented Porsche without an engine as a joke. In return, Newman had it crushed and left in a box at Redford's house!

Driving to the Beat

Porsches have inspired many musicians. In one classic tune, Janis Joplin sings, "My friends all drive Porsches." Joplin had a Porsche of her own. She painted her 1965 356C Cabriolet in the wild colors popular in the 1960s. Joplin's famous car has been on display at different art and auto museums all over the country.

In the song "Parents Just Don't Understand," Will Smith raps about sneaking out late one night in his parents' Porsche. He zips out for a little spin and gets pulled over "doing 90 in my mom's new Porsche."

INSIDE THE MACHINE

Lots of people think the Porsche is a real looker. Soon after the first Porsche arrived in the United States, its design caught the eye of the art world. In 1953, the Museum of Modern Art in New York City included a 1952 Porsche 1500 Super in one of its exhibits.

This famous photo of Janis Joplin and her Porsche was taken in the late 1960s.

Porsches on the Silver Screen

Plenty of Porsches have starred in movies through the years. In the 1971 movie *Le Mans,* actor and race-car enthusiast Steve McQueen drives a Porsche 917. McQueen races his Porsche against another race car—a Ferrari 512 LM—in a 24-hour race in France.

In *The Twilight Saga: New Moon* (2009), vampire Alice Cullen whips through Italy in a sunny yellow Porsche 911 Turbo. The animated film *Cars* (2006) features a character known as Sally Carerra. She is a light blue 2002 Porsche 911. The 1987 movie *No Man's Land* has many Porsches in it. A famous chase scene involves a 911.

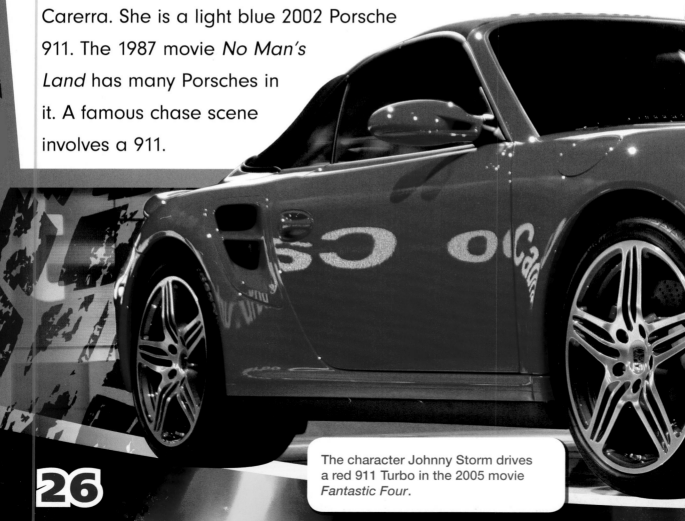

The character Johnny Storm drives a red 911 Turbo in the 2005 movie *Fantastic Four*.

INSIDE THE MACHINE

Comedian Jerry Seinfeld owns more Porsches than anyone else in the world. At one time he had 47 Porsches, including some rare models! He has one of only 200 Porsche 959s ever made. He even gave his wife a 1958 Porsche 1600 Speedster as a wedding present.

Exciting and Exotic

Porsche has a long history of making fresh and creative cars for the road and track. This company constantly pushes boundaries to make their automobiles faster, more powerful, and even more stunning. With a track record of nearly constant success, the future of Porsche cars is sure to be a thrilling ride!

The Porsche 918 RSR was introduced at the 2011 North American International Auto Show.

For More Information

Books

Bridges, Sarah. *Sports Cars*. Mankato, MN: Capstone Press, 2011.

Dredge, Richard. *World's Fastest Cars*. Sparkford, England: Haynes Publishing, 2010.

Walker, Robert. *Porsche*. New York, NY: Crabtree Publishing Company, 2011.

Websites

Collisionkids.org
www.collisionkids.org
Learn about cars by playing games and completing projects.

Porsche
www.porsche.com/usa/
Keep up with the latest Porsche models and racing news.

Porsche Family Tree
www.porschefamilytree.com/#/family-tree
Read stories and watch videos sent in by Porsche owners about their cars.

Index

INSIDE THE MACHINE

For some drivers, fast is just not fast enough. They want their Porsches to be the fastest! Here are some Porsches that have been specially tuned to tear up the track.

MODEL	TOP SPEED
9ff GT9 (911 GTS)	253 miles (407 km) per hour
H&R Mission 400 Plus (911 Turbo)	248 miles (400 km) per hour
9ff V-400 (911 Turbo)	241 miles (388 km) per hour
Sportec SPR1 (911 Turbo)	236 miles (380 km) per hour
Edo Competition Carrera GT	227 miles (365 km) per hour

Glossary

all-wheel drive: a system that uses all four wheels to drive a car instead of just the front or back wheels

carriage: a cart with wheels in which people can ride

convertible: a car with a roof that can be lowered or removed

coupe: a two-door car with one section for the seat and another for storage space

cylinder: the enclosed tube-shaped spaces where fuel is burned in an engine to create power

design: to create the pattern or shape of something. Also, the pattern or shape itself.

hybrid: a vehicle that runs on both gasoline and electricity

mid-ship engine: an engine located behind the passenger area but within the wheelbase. Also called a middie.

roadster: an open car with just two doors

roll bar: an overhead metal bar on an automobile that helps protect the driver in case of a rollover

symbol: a picture or object that stands for something else

turbocharger: a part that increases an engine's power

ventilation: movement of air in and through a space